THIS BOOK BELONGS TO :

_____

_____

_____

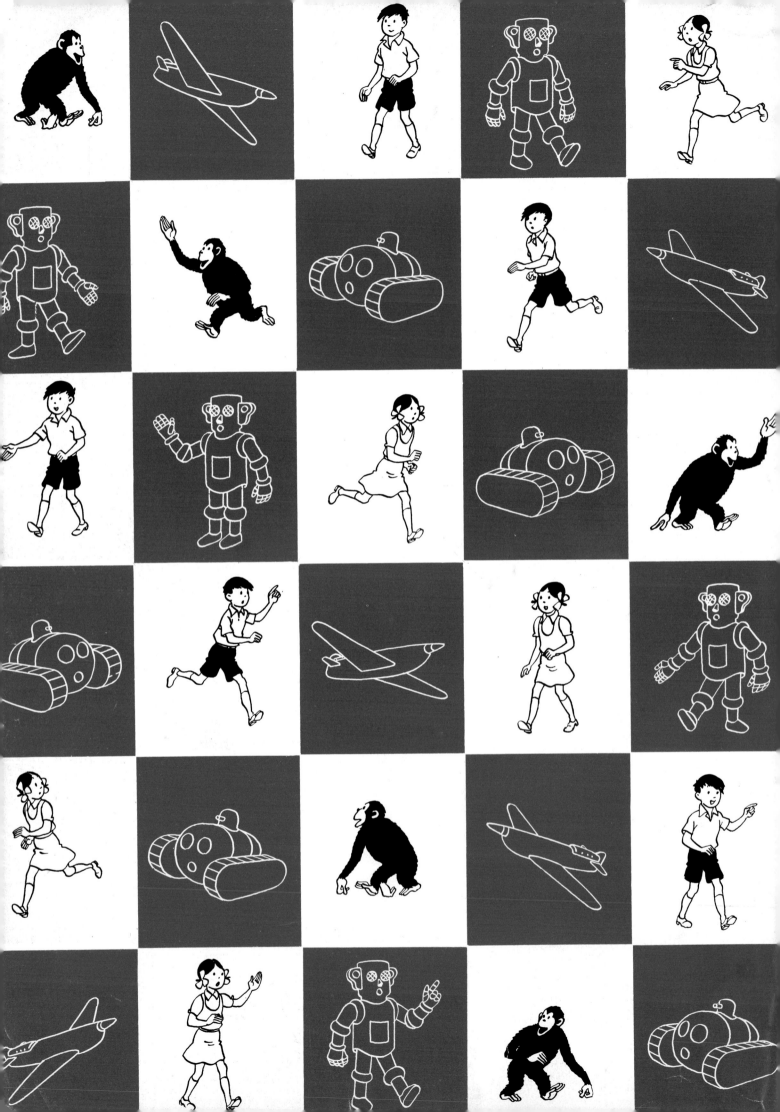

HERGÉ

THE ADVENTURES OF JO, ZETTE AND JOCKO

THE STRATOSHIP H. 22

PART TWO

DESTINATION NEW YORK

translated by Leslie Lonsdale-Cooper
and Michael Turner

The story so far, as told in: THE STRATOSHIP H.22
Part One: MR. PUMP'S LEGACY

An American Millionaire has left in his will ten million dollars to the builders of the first aeroplane to fly from Paris to New York non-stop at an average speed of 1000 kilometres per hour, the flight to be made within the year. To save the Stratoship H.22, designed by their father and now threatened by gangsters, Jo and Zette have taken off in the aircraft. Their pet monkey Jocko has gone too. Shortage of fuel forces them to land on an island ...

First published in English in 1987
by Methuen Children's Books Ltd.
Simultaneous Magnet paperback edition published 1987
Reissued 1990 by Mammoth,
an imprint of Egmont Children's Books Limited
239 Kensington High Street, London W8 6SL
Reprinted 1992, 1994 (twice) 1996, 1998.

Published in Belgium by Casterman, S.A.,
Rue des Sœurs Noires 28, B-7500 Tournai, Belgium
Copyright © 1951 by Casterman
© renewed 1979 by Casterman
Library of Congress Catalogue Card Numbers Afo 7447 and RE 45-462
All rights reserved
English translation by Leslie Lonsdale-Cooper and Michael Turner
Copyright © 1987 by Egmont Children's Books Ltd.

Printed by Casterman, S.A., Tournai, Belgium.

BRITISH LIBRARY CATALOGUING IN PUBLICATION DATA
Hergé
    Destination New York. — (The Adventures of
Jo, Zette and Jocko)
    I. Title   II. Series   III. Destination
New York. *English*
741.5'9493   PN6790.B43H4

ISBN 0-416-01532-8
ISBN 0-7497-0531-0 Pbk

DESTINATION NEW YORK

There!... My report will go by the next boat.

Let's see, when will the next boat be passing?... Well...The last one came a month ago... So the next will be here in five months, since there are two a year...

Consequently, in five months the report will go. Six months later it will come back, with orders from the government... That means...five plus six... eleven... In eleven months you will know your fate...

YEOWWW

YEOWW

Ha! ha! ha! ha!

YEOWWW

? A storm!

To the Stratoship, quick!... We can shelter there!

One of the mechanics must have left his flask and sandwiches in the aircraft.

Lucky for us... I don't know what we'd have eaten otherwise.

The storm rages all night...

Next morning...

Oh!... Look there, Zette!... Oil drums!

There must have been a shipwreck last night ...And the storm cast the wreckage ashore...

Let's roll one up the beach. We'll see what's inside.

We're saved, Zette! ... It's full of petrol!

Quick! Something to put it in ... We'll fill the tanks!

Let's see what's in those barrels...

?

Funny, it doesn't smell of anything...

BOOM

Petrol!... Full of petrol! ...And because of this bandage, I couldn't smell it!

Let him go... Let's get on filling the tanks...

Slow going, isn't it, Jo?

I know, but with a little patience we'll do it.

By that evening...

That's it!... Now we can leave...

But Jo, have you any idea which way we ought to go?

Which way?... I... er... I mean... That's to say...

...Not exactly. But the island we just left can't have been far from the equator... Or for that matter, far south of Europe. So I'm going to steer towards the north, following the compass.

Meanwhile...

Hello?... Is that the Air Ministry? ...This is Jacques Legrand...Still no news?...Nothing?...Yes...You'll keep me informed?...Thank you...

Oh! There's a ship!... How small it looks... Just like a toy...

Good heavens! It's the plane they said was missing...The Stratoship H.22!

Hello...Hello...This is SS Anversville calling... 2017 hours... Position 19°40 W, 4°26 N. Aircraft Stratoship H.22 sighted flying at high altitude, steering northerly course...

RRRRING
RRRRING

Hello?...Yes...The Air Ministry... Yes...You have news?...They... they're alive!...Heaven be praised! ...Sighted by SS Anversville? ...Going where?...Due north!... But...if they don't change course they'll miss Europe ...

It's getting dark again... Still no sight of land...

Still nothing...Not even the lights of a city...

Perhaps it's foggy, Jo...

RRRING
RRING

Hello?... Air Ministry here...Yes... yes... We've had word from Reykjavik, in Iceland, saying that at three o'clock in the morning, an hour ago, the people of Dyrholaey, on the southern coast, heard the sound of an aircraft engine...   heading north...

Heading north!... They're done for!... They're going straight for the Arctic!

Courage, Zette ...It will soon be getting light...

The dawn is coming ...

Just as well, since we're running short of fuel again...

Ah! I can just begin to see something...I...Oh, Jo!... It's all white!... It's snow!...

At this time of year?

Golly, Zette!... We've come too far! It's the North Pole!

We must turn round and go back towards the south.

We wouldn't get very far... Look at the fuel gauge: only a few litres left!...

I'll try, anyway!... If only we could see an Eskimo settlement.

Nothing... Nothing... We really must land...

There's an icefield smooth enough to be a landing strip...

Is it?...

Watch out, Jo... The surface is all bumpy!

CRACK

?

The undercarriage is smashed!

The propeller's crumpled!

What will become of us?

Good gracious!... It looks... But it's too far away... It looks ...Yes!... They're people!... We're saved!

We're still too far. They won't hear you.

AHOY!...AHOY!

Brr!... It's jolly cold!

They'll certainly be Eskimos ...

Oh!... I can't see them now!

Keep going, Zette... We're nearly there...

Listen!...You can hear them talking...They're behind that cliff.

Yes. Eskimo is a funny language!

? ? !

ARRH   EURRH   iiRRH

RAAH!   EURRH!

Penguins!...

No, they're guillemots... They looked like people from a distance.

Jocko!... Come here!

In a minute!

Back to the plane ...

I don't much care for eggs, but I'm dying of hunger, and beggars can't be choosers!

ARRH!   RRAH!

?

We must hurry! The weather is worsening.
Yes, the wind is getting up.

Jocko?...
¡¡RRH! EURRH!

Quick!... Quick!
Perhaps he's being attacked by a bear!

Oh!... Poor old Jocko!

It's starting to snow.
Let's hurry, Jo. I'm freezing.

It's a real blizzard!
I can't see anything ahead.

Where's the aeroplane?... I can't see it now...

Don't worry, Zette, we'll find it... It can't be far away.
I hope so. I can't go much further...

We've lost our way!
Oh Jo! We'll die of cold!

Don't give up!... We'll go down again and keep on searching...

Jocko?...
He's slipped!
WHAA

Jocko!...Jocko! He's disappeared!

Oh! Oh! What will happen to him?

CRACK

Come on, Zette! Be brave!

Zette!...Zette!... You must keep going ...You'll get numb with cold.

I can't go further, Jo. Leave me ... try to save your-self.

He seems to want to take you out-side...

Yes...Perhaps there are people in danger...I'm going to follow him.

Wait a minute... I'll wrap him in something warm.

Good idea.

Come on, Zette, keep going! We'll walk back-wards, then we won't have the snow in our faces...

That's better, isn't it?

Yes...

Footprints!...Two of them... Look like children...They went that way...

Here we are.

That's better!

But the transatlantic flight, Zette!... How can it succeed now...with only three weeks left?... And the plane is damaged.

I know, Jo... there's little hope now...

Let's try to explain to them we can't stay long, and somehow or other we must try to get in touch with our parents.

Er...we come by aeroplane... Flying machine ...Rrrrrrrrrr...You understand?... We come down... Bzzzzz

And suddenly... Crrack... Bang...

In fact, as I understand it, you wanted to land, but instead of touching down like a feather, you came a cropper...

Yes! I was taught your language by an ethnologist, Professor Nielsen ...As soon as the weather clears we will go to see him. He has a radio transmitter. He'll be able to use it to reassure your parents.

The storm rages for three days...

On the fourth morning...

Today the weather is better. We can set out.   But first we must find some   food for the journey...

We will go out seal-hunting.

What super slides they have round here.

13

Ooh! The ice floe is leaving the shore!

An hour later...

He's probably back home already...

Jocko!

Jocko?

Jocko?... No... He followed when you went out earlier...

He'll be somewhere around. He'll turn up. Meantime, I will prepare the sledge.

Help! Help!... I'm drifting further and further from the shore...

The sledge is ready. There's no time to be lost. We don't want to be caught by another snowstorm.

You are right... We must go.

My poor Jocko!... I shall never see you again...

The coast has disappeared!... I'm right out at sea!

If the weather holds we'll reach Professor Nielsen in two days.

Unfortunately the sky is growing dark again. We shall have snow before nightfall.

What did I tell you... Our journey is going to be badly delayed.

We can't go on. The dogs are exhausted. We must stop and build an igloo...

When we've finished this, we'll build another igloo for the dogs.

Two days the storm has been blowing...Two days lost, Zette.

Yes... It seems to me our flight has less and less chance...

And our poor parents!...What they must be suffering!

Hello?...Air Ministry?... This is Jacques Legrand ...No... Still nothing?... Yes... Thank you.

And poor Jocko! Where can he be now?

Jo!...Zette!... Jocko is hungry!... Jocko is starving to death!

16

That's a ship's siren!... It must be quite close... Without this horrid fog I'd have seen it...

Ooh!... Look out!

Iceberg!... Dead ahead!

Port!... Hard to port!...

Do your best to calm the passengers. I'll try to see what the damage is.

Luckily the impact was well above the waterline... There is no immediate danger.

Resume your course at slow speed. I'm going to radio a report of the accident.

It's OK... According to the radio message I'm sending, the damage won't hold us up...

Captain, look what we found in the galley! ...This villain! He ate a whole bunch of bananas, and was asleep in the fast locker!

It must belong to one of the passengers... Fetch the purser.

No, Captain, none of the passengers embarked with a monkey.

How very odd... And look, he's dressed in furs, like an Eskimo.

The only possible answer is that this monkey was on the iceberg we hit just now, and the impact threw him on board.

But what was he doing on the iceberg?

He seems friendly, and very intelligent...

What shall we do with him, sir?

Look after him till we get to New York. We'll decide there. If you like, you can keep him as a mascot.

A mascot!

A mascot!... A mascot who eats our entire stock of bananas!... I don't need that sort of mascot in my galley!

What if we teach him to wash up?

?

OH!

OH!

Saved!...They look like friends!

Good gracious!... Is it mad?

⁉

No, it just wanted to give you a hug!

Aha! There it is! Wretched animal, you'll be sorry you led us a dance!

Is this your monkey?

Mine?...

Yes and no...I mean, the monkey was on the iceberg we ran into earlier on. It was catapulted on board, and the Captain gave it to me.

A monkey on an iceberg... Seems very odd to me...

Wait while I look at him...Why... Good heavens! It could be... Yes! It's Jocko!

It's Jocko, Clare!...You know, the monkey that went with Jo and Zette Legrand when they flew off in the Stratoship.

So it is!... How pleased he is to be recognised!

I assure you, Captain, it certainly is Jocko. Compare him with the photograph in the newspaper.

20

Get the radio officer here at once!

SS Oceanic 1528 hours in passage to New York. Position 43°26 W, 48°31 N. We have aboard monkey answering to name Jocko Stop We believe belongs to Jo and Zette Legrand Stop Found on iceberg rammed by us Stop Monkey dressed in Eskimo furs Stop

Meanwhile...

Hello?... Yes...The Air Ministry?...Yes...Yes...Aah! They are safe?...What?...Only Jocko?... Jocko?...On an iceberg...dressed like an Eskimo?

Yes...It leads one to suppose that Jo and Zette have also been rescued by Eskimos...And to hope that they are safe and well.

The storm is over. We can be on our way.

Not far now. All being well, we'll be at the camp tonight.

...and that evening...

Look, Professor, a sledge.

Greetings, Professor!

Ah!...It's Iriouk... Greetings Iriouk! You brought your children?

No, Professor, they are two French children.

French children?!

Jo and Zette Legrand from Paris ...we were saved by Iriouk.

Jo and Zette Legrand?...You piloted the Stratoship H.22? ...Everyone thought you were lost!...How good to see you safe and sound!...Quick, we must radio the news of your rescue at once! ...Come with me.

This is KR2 calling...This is KR2 calling...Come in PGM...Come in PGM.

PGM receiving you...PGM receiving you...Go ahead KR2...

KR2 calling...KR2 calling...Please inform Reykjavik South that Jo and Zette Legrand, who piloted Stratoship H.22, just arrived safe and well at KR2, after being picked up by Eskimos...

Wait a minute. PGM will reply. Ah!... Now!

PGM to KR2... PGM to KR2... We are informing Reykjavik South... Stand by, please... Stand by...

Reykjavik South to PGM...We have informed Paris FR6... Please connect KR2...

Reykjavik South to KR2... Please stand by... Paris FR6 wishes to speak to you...

PARIS!

Paris FR6 calling KR2...Paris calling KR2...Are you receiving me?... Are you receiving me?

In a moment you can speak to them...

Jo!...Zette!...Can you hear me? ...Can you hear me?...This is Papa!

Papa!...Hello!...Yes!... Hello, Papa!...Yes...No... Not a bit!...Zette and I are both very well...Yes... But we lost Jocko!...What? ...He's been found!... That's wonderful!

Jo, tell me...Is the Stratoship badly damaged?...Yes...I see ...That's all?...The undercarriage smashed and the propeller bent...Good...That isn't very serious...

S.A.F.C.A. will fit out an aeroplane to bring the necessary spare parts. As soon as the repairs are complete we'll return to Paris. There'll be enough time, I hope, to make the Paris–New York flight before the dead-line.

Goodbye, Papa...See you soon!... Give our love to Mama...And tell her not to worry any more... Everyone here is very kind...The Eskimos are terribly nice people, and they speak English just like us!

That's it!... We're off the air... Now we just have to wait for the relief plane.

Meanwhile in Paris...

Hello?... Yes... This is the "Dispatch" ... Yes... Excellent!... Well done!... They've been found!... Good!... Hold on, my secretary will take it down...

"A message received from Radio Station KR2, relayed via Reykjavik, confirms that the two Legrand children have been found and are safe and well."

All done?... Good!... Take it to the newsroom... I want that on the front page, across four columns, instead of the trial of the Dalmatian terrorists...

Daily Dispatch!... Daily Dispatch!... Special... Special!

"...S.A.F.C.A. immediately decided to send a relief aircraft to make any necessary repairs on the spot. They are confident they will meet the deadline for a successful transatlantic flight..." Confound it!

Those children have the luck of the devil, curse them!... Anyone else would have smashed themselves to bits!... Now thanks to them, S.A.F.C.A. can still scoop the jackpot!

There's still a way to spike their guns... Go tonight...

To see Victor, eh?... The foreman at S.A.F.C.A.

That night...

Hello, Victor!

Werner!

Ssh!... Not so loud!... Victor, we have a little job for you...

You know that S.A.F.C.A. are sending an aircraft to rescue the Stratoship... You, my dear Victor, will see that aeroplane does not reach its destination.

23

No! No! No! ... This time I've had enough! ... All right, I sabotaged the Stratoship for you before the test flight ... But I don't want to re-live those hours I went through, waiting for news of the crash... Never!

Come on, don't be difficult! ... There's ten thousand dollars in it for you...

I won't! ... I've had enough! ... Why do you hate Legrand, anyway?

That's my business! ... One last time ... Will you do it?

No!

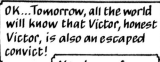

OK...Tomorrow, all the world will know that Victor, honest Victor, is also an escaped convict!

You know I didn't do it...

Well?...

All right. What do you want?

Two days later...

There... From Paris to Reykjavik, the first leg, is about 4000 kilometres...All being well we can there by tonight.

Everything ready, Victor?

I...Yes, sir. I've checked it all.

The second leg, from Reykjavik to station KR2 will be more difficult...

Your father's plane was here at 1135 GMT...They left Scotland and headed for Iceland...

There... they are there...

Visibility excellent. Speed 375 km/h. All well... Next report at 1300 hours.

1257...three more minutes...

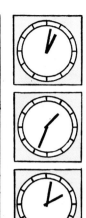

Still no report...

Let's hope nothing has happened to them!

Oh, Papa!

Hello?... Air Ministry? ...This is Madame Legrand...Is there any news?

Sadly not, Madame. Nothing at all. But there is still hope...A full search is being made...

...This is Radio Paris at 2200 hours. There is still no news of the S.A.F.C.A. trimotor aircraft. Royal The search mounted by the Air Force was called off at nightfall but will be resumed at first light...

Victor did a good job ...

You mustn't give up hope. We don't know they are lost. Their radio could be out of order...

Poor, poor Papa!

Listen...Tomorrow morning we'll go in my aeroplane... We'll try to locate the Strato-ship and examine the damage...If it can be repaired on the spot we'll do it.

The next morning...

This is the little plane I use to move around the territory.

Meanwhile...

Wreckage to starboard!

An aircraft wing!

Trawler D 239...0548 hours...11°38 West, 66°12 North...We have recovered aircraft wing, registration I G A.

Hello? This is the Air Ministry...Yes...A trawler? ...IGA...The trimotor's registration!...They are lost! ...Heavens! How can I tell Madame Legrand?

There's the Strato-ship...Down to the right?

Oh, I thought it would be worse...

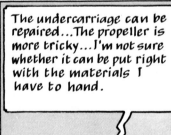

Is it serious?

The undercarriage can be repaired...The propeller is more tricky...I'm not sure whether it can be put right with the materials I have to hand.

We must go back to base ...We'll collect the men and the materials we need and send them here...

There goes Professor Nielsen's plane.

The Professor is back already.

I need a dozen men and four sledges to salvage an aircraft lying eighty miles from here, a few miles from Iriouk's igloo... Is that possible?

Yes, Professor. All will be ready tomorrow.

Next morning...
Goodbye, Narak, and good luck!... We will come by aeroplane and join you there tomorrow evening.

If they don't manage to repair the Stratoship we can say goodbye to the Atlantic crossing, Zette... There are only twelve days left...

Meanwhile...

Two days since we were picked up by these fishermen, just as we were sinking...

And without a radio aboard, impossible to let anyone know what's happened...

Hello, there's the skipper!

Well, Captain, when do we arrive?

If the wind doesn't change we'll be in Kirkwall tomorrow evening.

The next afternoon...

Here comes the Professor and his two young passengers...

So?... A good journey?... Yes?... And the Stratoship?

Fine. We have already righted it...

...and our two engineers have started work.

Excellent!

Another day gone by, and still no news of Papa!

Poor Papa!... Where is he now?

There's the coast!... At last we can pass on our news...

Hello?...This is the Air Ministry ...Yes...Hello? Who is that?... What?... Legrand!...You!... Safe and well!... Saved by a fishing boat?!

Where are you?...Where? ...Kirkwall...The Orkney Islands...Off northern Scotland...I... I'll tell Madame Legrand at once!

Hello?...Yes, this is Madame Legrand...Yes ...Safe!...Praise be!

...Tomorrow evening the Stratoship will be ready to fly again. But...who will pilot it?

Why, us, Professor!

Next day...

There! The undercarriage is repaired.

Marvellous! But what about the propeller?

The propeller?... We just have to fit the new one. That won't take long...

The new one?... A new propeller?... I...I don't understand.

Here!...I remembered, I kept the propeller from my first aeroplane. With a few modifications it fits the Strato-ship very well.

As soon as they've finished, we'll return to base. I will fly the Stratoship and Narak will bring my aeroplane.

One last can of fuel, and we're all ready.

Now, I'm going to start the engine. If all is well, you come aboard...I'm planning to take you to France.

? ?

Hooray!

Hooray!

Professor!...Baby Loumak is ill and her mother has been calling for you since yesterday!...And the old medicine man Iriakouk is dying...

Very well! I'll come at once...

Did you hear what he said? He wants to fly the Stratoship to France... But we can't accept that, Zette... You can see how much he is needed here...

Listen, Zette...This is my idea... While he's away we'll take the chance to refuel and go... What do you think?

I think you're right, Jo. We can't allow him to leave his job here...

Right!... We must be quick, before he comes back. We'll leave him a letter to explain why we went off so suddenly.

Yes...

Heavens!

This time, Jo, don't go the wrong way...

Don't worry, Zette, I studied the map well. We must head south-east.

Some hours later...

Land, Zette!... Land!

How wonderful!

Look!... An aeroplane!

I'd say it's going to land...

He's landed!...

Let's have a look ...

Look at the people! I think we're in France!

HOTEL NORM

Werner! I've found you at last!

What's the matter? You look upset...

Werner, the Stratoship just landed on the beach...

What?...Don't talk rubbish...You're crazy!

I'm not crazy, Werner!...It's the Stratoship, there on the beach!... And I saw Jo and Zette get out!

Curse them!

Meanwhile...

RRRRING

Hello?...Yes...Yes it is ...Who?...Thank goodness! Jo!...Jo!...Is it really you, Jo?...

Yes, it's me, Mama! ...And Zette is here, too...Yes, we're very much alive!...Where? ...At Dunes-les-Bains ...A few minutes ago ...And Papa?...

Papa returned from Scotland this morning ...He's here...I'll hand you over...

Jo?...We'll come now!... Yes!...In two hours we'll be at Dunes-les-Bains... And don't forget to have the Stratoship guarded... Already done?...Good!

Meanwhile...
Ssh!...Careful...The plane is sure to be guarded...

Look!...Police!...I knew they'd be there...

Leave the petrol can here. Bring your cosh and follow me...

Quick!...Go and fetch the petrol...

We'll be there in a few minutes.

That's it!...Pour the lot!... We want the stuff well soaked with petrol...

One end pushed into the fuel tank, a lighted match at the other end, and the Stratoship is a has-been!

There!...That's it!... Give me your matches!

Devil take him!
Some fire extinguisher!

Jo!

Thank heavens! Papa is safe!

Hooray!

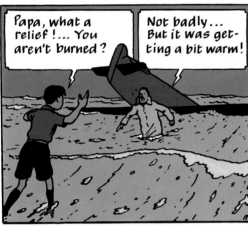

Papa, what a relief!... You aren't burned?

Not badly... But it was getting a bit warm!

The main thing is, we saved the Stratoship!... At low tide we'll haul it clear...

Let's get out!

Wait, it's too good a chance!

BANG

Missed!... Now they're taking cover.

-BANG
-BANG

All over?

I think so...

To the hotel, quick!... Then back to Paris!

Thank heavens, another attempt misfired...Patience, Jo! We'll win through in spite of it all...

This is Radio Paris... In a few moments we shall be bringing you live coverage of the departure of the Stratoship H.22 ...As reported, there have been numerous attacks on the aircraft... Only last week the plane was almost destroyed by fire...Engineer Legrand managed to save the machine, which was brought to Paris next day...Since then the Stratoship has been overhauled and is ready...

...Today at last it will be taking to the air and making its 1000 km/h Atlantic crossing... It is still unclear why the gangsters tried so desperately to destroy the aircraft... Reports confirm that theories of sabotage by a rival company can be discounted... The mystery remains...Whatever the answer, the time of departure has arrived, so I am handing you over to our reporter at the airfield...

Well, here we are at the airfield, where, in a few minutes, the Stratoship H.22 will take off ...It is 7.30 am. The crowd, very large despite the early hour, is being kept at a distance by a police cordon. Security guards ring the aircraft. Overhead, military planes are on patrol...The Stratoship is well protected...

Not far away I can see Engineer Legrand's children. Like us, they are waiting for their father... We know that at this very moment he and the pilot are receiving a last-minute briefing from the director of S.A.F.C.A. ...

Well, Zette!... A few hours and the prize will be won!

This time the end really is in sight.

...So! Here's to your victory, gentlemen! ...

...Departure was fixed for eight o'clock and it is now nearly nine. The Stratoship crew still haven't arrived...The anxious crowd is becoming restive.

I wonder what they're doing...

Let's see...

In here...

No answer... That's funny...

Oh Jo... I'm afraid...

? ?

Papa!... What's the matter?... Answer me!...

Quick Zette!... Run!... We must get a doctor!

!

Quick, doctor!... I think they've been drugged!

You're quite right... These men are under the influence of a powerful soporific...

Doctor... Will they be asleep for long?

That depends which narcotic was used.

...No danger of them coming round. We used a very strong preparation ...almost unknown...

But the flight, doctor!... The deadline expires on the 25th... In three days!

I'll do my best, my very best, but ...

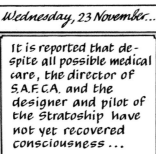

Wednesday, 23 November...

It is reported that despite all possible medical care, the director of S.A.F.C.A. and the designer and pilot of the Stratoship have not yet recovered consciousness ...

Thursday, 24 November...

The condition of the three victims remains stable. In aviation circles it is rumoured that the flight is to be abandoned.

...And the deadline for the attempt expires at midnight tomorrow...

Poor Papa!... All these months working flat out, only to be defeated at the last minute!

Zette!... Listen!... If Papa isn't better by tomorrow morning I'll pilot the Stratoship myself and I'll fly it to New York!

Jo!...

What if young Jo takes it into his head to fly the Stratoship himself, by any chance? He's shown he is capable of it...

Don't worry, I thought of that. I've taken precautions...

Next morning at dawn . . .

He's still deeply unconscious...

Poor, poor Papa!

Come on, Zette, let's go! ...We've no choice...

What about the letter for Mama Where is it?

There, on my bed...

Come along, Zette!... All or nothing, now!

One of Werner's bright ideas!...Gets us to watch the house in case the kids sneak off with the Strato-ship!

Oh!...Hey!...Look!...The gate is opening...

The kids!...They're going out!

Quick, they've already gone round the corner...

?

Drat!...They've ta- ken a taxi!

Now what?...We must follow them...

But there isn't another taxi!

?

RRRING RRRING RRRING

Hello?...Hello?...Yes...Oh, it's you?...What!...By thunder!... Given the slip by a couple of children!... Imbeciles!

They must be stopped at all costs!

The main gate is closed. We must go round the perimeter...

Come on! I can't see anyone...

Halt!

? ?

Oh, it's you? What do you want, so early?

It's old Jules, the watchman!

Er... Good morning Jules... We... You see... Papa has recovered, and he's coming here... He wants the Stratoship rolled out... He... We... I mean, the flight is going ahead today.

Stay here... I'll go and tell the ground crew...

Sorry, Jules... I had to get rid of you... Quick, the plane!

Meanwhile ...

40

Oh, Madame Legrand...Thank... thank you for...coming...I...I have done so much harm...to you and to Monsieur Legrand.

Now... I am dying...I want you to know everything... It was Mr Pump's nephews... William and Fred Stockrise... who wanted...at all costs... to stop...

...the flight of the Stratoship... You remember...If within a year of the will... the crossing hadn't been made... the legacy... ten million dollars... would go to the nephews.

So...They promised me a lot of money...to sabotage the aircraft... or destroy it... I accepted ...

... and I failed...The flight will succeed, I am sure ...

Alas, that is impossible...The deadline expires tonight and neither my husband nor the pilot has recovered con- sciousness

But... But you don't know? Jo and Zette have already gone...

What did you say ?... Jo and Zette ?

Gone... in the Stratoship...Yes... I ... Now you know everything...Can you forgive me ?

I forgive you.

Meanwhile ...

It is 8.30 am. It was 6.10 am when we left...

Good... Let's hope I don't deviate from my course ...

Meanwhile ...

9 o'clock !... I wonder what's happened to Werner ...

Yes... He should have been back here ages ago...

RAT
TAT
TAT ?

William Stockrise?...

I... Yes... that's me... What do you want?

I arrest you in the name of the law!

Look out!

A little later...

It is disgraceful! I am an American citizen and I protest!

Perhaps you will protest a little less when you know that Werner has confessed...

Werner confessed?... All right... So it was me ... I did all I could to stop the flight planned by S.A.F.C.A. I needed that money promised by my uncle...

As soon as I knew what was in the will I came to France where I met an old pal, Charlie Brooke, from my Chicago days. He put me in touch with Werner. And things haven't gone too badly, have they? The deadline expires tonight, and the Stratoship is grounded...

That's what you think!... At this moment the Stratoship is heading for America!

?

This is Paris FR6... This is Paris FR6... Calling New York Central... New York Central...

Paris FR6 to New York Central... Stratoship H.22, piloted by Jo and Zette, left Paris this morning at 6.00 am local time, destination New York...

This is New York Central... Message received...

Look at the indicator, Zette! We are doing over 1000 km/h.

At this speed I'm sure we can't be very far from the American coast, Zette.

This is Radio New York Central... News has just come in that the French aircraft Stratoship H.22 left Paris around 6.00 am local time today in the Paris-New York record attempt... To win the prize offered under the will of millionaire John A. Pump, the plane must cover the distance, about 3750 miles, in under six hours...

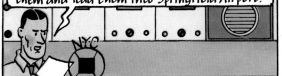
The time difference between Paris and New York is five hours, so our calculations tell us that the plane should land here in New York around seven o'clock... This event is unprecedented in aviation history... The Stratoship is piloted by Jo Legrand, with his little sister Zette riding along ...To help the two youngsters, several fighter squadrons have taken off, to meet them and lead them into Springfield Airport.

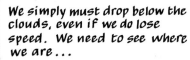

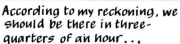
According to my reckoning, we should be there in three-quarters of an hour...

Yes, if we're on the right course.

We simply must drop below the clouds, even if we do lose speed. We need to see where we are...

The sea! Still the sea!

No!... Down there!... The American coast, Zette!

America!

Meanwhile, in New York...

The time is now precisely six thirty...The planes sent to meet the Stratoship still report no sighting of the aircraft...

43

Look! There she is!...

Zette!... An aeroplane!... Down there, it's turning!

This is F-147... Stratoship in sight... Squadrons B-31, B-32 and B-35 turn 180 degrees... Form line ahead...500 feet intervals... Heading Springfield Airport.

Jo!... Jo!... I've got it!... He's showing us the way...You just have to follow their line.

Saved!

Oh! There's another one... And another... Look how fast we're overtaking them!

You understand?... Twenty-five thousand dollars if you pull it off!

OK, Mister Fred Stockrise!... Don't you worry!...This is just my sort of stunt!

He's some flyer!... Film studios always hire him when they need to shoot a scene of an air crash...

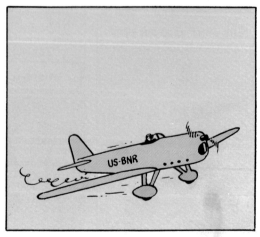

Ah!... There's a plane!... And another...

Lousy Army Air Force fighters... Too bad... They won't have time to interfere!

Ah! The famous Stratoship!

I mustn't goof!... At this speed it's quite a job!

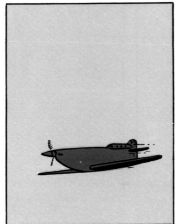

We're getting near... I'm going to reduce speed a little...

Yes, mind we don't overshoot the airfield...

In a dive I'll easily gain enough speed...

Here we go!... Take good aim!

We're there Zette!... I can see the field...

Missed!

Quick! Get her nose up!... Come on!... Otherwise...

What the...?! She won't answer to the stick!...

Hey!... Look!... A guy going down in a spin!

The Stratoship! Here it comes!... Hooray!

Don't forget the wheels, will you, Jo!

Don't worry, Zette!... There!...I've done it!...

The Stratoship is preparing to land ...Almost touching down...Oh! I can't believe it... They haven't put down their landing gear ...

As I speak to you, the Stratoship has hurtled into the ground and disappeared in a cloud of smoke...

ABC

The poor kids!

Oh, the children!

What happened?

The undercarriage didn't come down...

They're alive!...

Hooray!

Long live Jo and Zette!

?

Jocko!

Meanwhile, in Paris...

Heavens!...What happened?... Where am I?...I can't remember... Oh, yes!... The flight!...

The 25th... It's the 25th ... So we've failed!

Here is the news...The Stratoship landed in New York at 6.57am local time. It covered the distance from Paris at an average speed of 1029 km/h.

I'll get my revenge!

The parade has just moved off... The crowds massed along the route are going crazy with excitement. It's a rousing reception for the two young aviators...

...They are arriving now at City Hall. The Mayor of New York steps forward with an address of welcome...

...All America salutes you! You, the heroes of the epoch-making stratospheric Paris-New York record flight. Proud representatives of the youth of France...

As the representative of every American schoolchild it is my privilege to offer you these flowers...

...Following the reception held in their honour, Jo and Zette Legrand have gone to the Imperial Hotel. They will stay there until they return to their own country ...

Whew!... Now we can have a rest... I'm really beginning to feel tired, Zette!

Me too, Jo!... Peace at last!

The press are asking whether Mister Jo and Miss Zette will receive them.

The press?...Oh, I suppose so... Please let them in...

48

How did you feel during the flight?

Do you like icecream?

Do you play with dolls?

Mister Jo, there are people here asking for your autographs...

Autographs? ...Very well, we'll come...

At this moment the two young aviators are signing autographs for the crowd at their hotel...

Ah!... That's an idea!

Now I've got them!

Quick! To their hotel!

I'm not too late!

I just have to wait my turn...

Your autograph, please, Mr Jo...

And now Miss Zette... Thank you!

There... Unfold the paper... and that's the ticket!

We, the undersigned, Jo and Zette Legrand, admit that we flew from the Azores, where the Stratoship H.22 was secretly taken by sea

Jo Zette

I'll give this to Herbert Jones, the journalist... We'll have the last laugh!

Next morning...

THE DISPATCH

A blatant fraud!

STRATOSHIP H.22 FLEW FROM AZORES

This startling revelation was made today by reporter Herbert Jones, who says he has absolute proof to back his claim. In making this extraordinary disclosure Herbert Jones has certainly

...Jo and Zette were immediately placed under arrest and are in custody...

Don't let's be too depressed, Zette ... It won't be hard to prove we are telling the truth.

Hello... Are we being released?

No, you're going to be questioned by the District Attorney.

Do you admit you signed this paper?

They certainly are our signatures, sir... But I promise you we never signed any such declaration!

So?... You still claim you flew from Paris?

Absolutely!... And it won't be hard to prove!

50

Good!...Thank you... You'll be taken to your cell...Your statement will be checked.

Cable Paris right away. Ask them to launch an immediate inquiry to discover if the Stratoship really left Paris on the date and time claimed by Jo and Zette Legrand.

Some hours later...

Here's the reply from the French authorities...

That's good!...They were telling the truth... Have someone fetch the reporter who started this business ...

We need to have the name of the person who gave you this document.

I'm sorry, Mr Attorney, but you know I can't reveal my sources...

I understand...But this document is a fake... If you don't tell me who wrote it I'll have you arrested!

Well, in that case I'll tell you : it's Fred Stockrise.

Fred Stockrise ...Thank you... That gentleman will be put under arrest right away!

An hour later...

You are free!

You!

D'you know who that is? ...It's Fred Stockrise, the guy who cooked up the fake document accusing you.

Oh! The gangster!

Jocko!...Jocko!...

OW YEOW

51

THE FLIGHT OF STRATOSHIP H.22
New York, Wednesday

All the formalities have now been completed, and young Jo and Zette Legrand have taken possession of Mr Pump's legacy of ten million dollars. With their faithful Jocko they embarked today aboard the SS Champlain, bound for Cherbourg.
We learned that Fred Stockrise has admitted responsibility for all the attacks directed against Mr Legrand and his family, and against the Stratoship H.22. He and his brother William were immediately charged with a string of crimes.

THE FLIGHT OF STRATOSHIP H.22
Paris, Monday

When SS Champlain docked at Cherbourg yesterday afternoon Monsieur and Madame Legrand were on the quay to meet their children. The young aviators were given an ecstatic welcome.
On arrival in Paris this morning, they were officially received by the President of the Republic. He congratulated them warmly upon their resolution, energy and courage, demonstrated by the successful Paris – New York flight.

THE FLIGHT OF STRATOSHIP H.22
Paris, Wednesday

After a short rest, Jo and Zette Legrand this morning bought a magnificent motor caravan equipped with every modern device
Talking to reporters who asked if they now planned to use this form of transport, Jo and Zette told them that the caravan was intended for a family of gipsies.
This story goes back to the night when the Stratoship airfield was bombed.

THE FIGHT OF STRATOSHIP H.22
Paris, Sunday

It has been confirmed that Jo and Zette Legrand have purchased a long range transport aircraft with a top speed of over 400 km/h. This machine, specially equipped for use in polar regions, has a convertible undercarriage which can be adapted for skis. It took off this morning for an undisclosed destination.
It is believed that the aircraft is a gift for an ethnologist who assisted Jo and Zette Legrand.

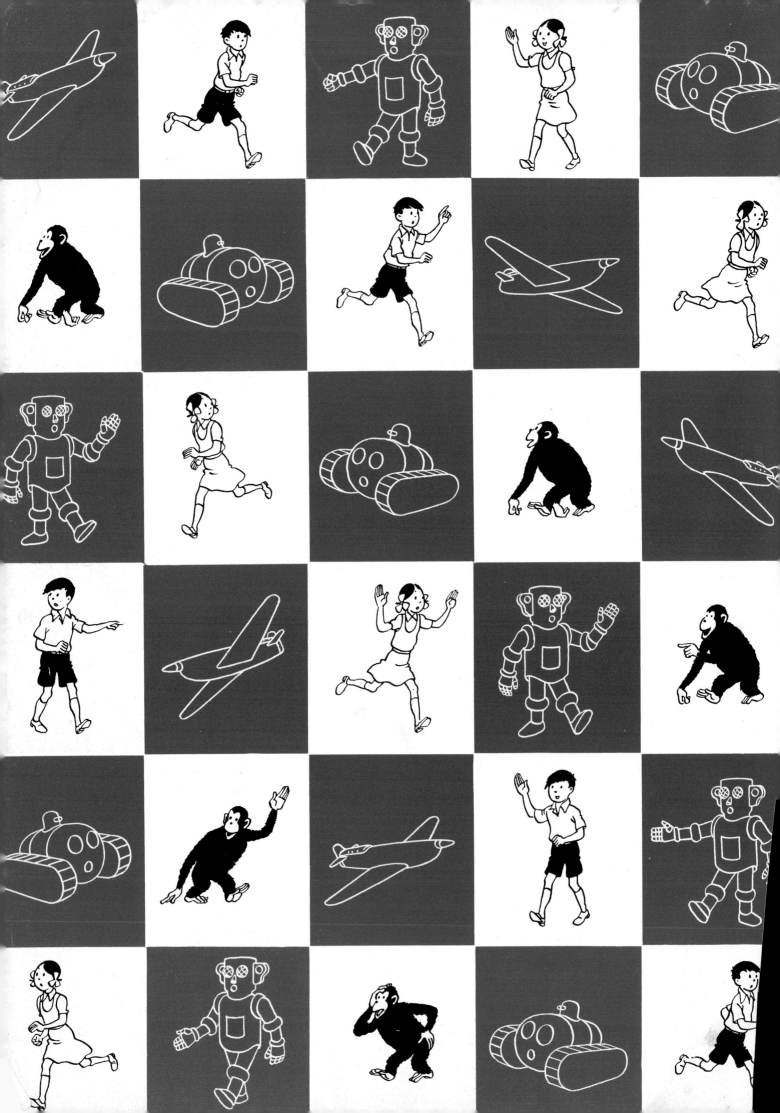

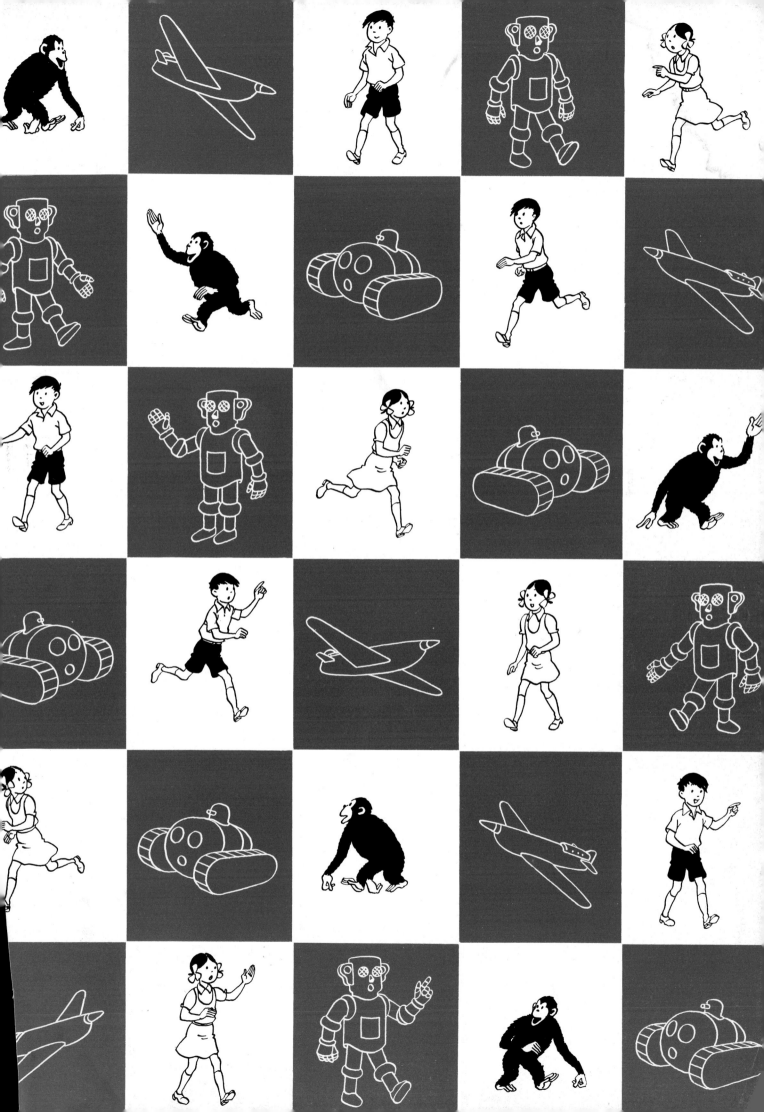